Happy to be Me

Bobbie Kalman

The In My World Series

Toronto
New York
Crabtree Publishing Company

The In My World Series
Conceived and coordinated by Bobbie Kalman

Writing team:
Bobbie Kalman
Susan Hughes
Diane Cook-Brissenden

Editors:
Susan Hughes
Ruth Chernia

Cover and title page design:
Oksana Ruczenczyn, Leslie Smart and Associates

Design and mechanicals:
Ruth Chernia

Illustrations:
Title page by Karen Harrison © Crabtree Publishing Company 1985
Pages 28-32 by Deborah Drew-Brook-Cormack
© Crabtree Publishing Company 1985
Pages 4-29 and cover © Mitchell Beazley Publishers 1982

Cataloging in Publication Data

Kalman, Bobbie, 1947–
    Happy to be me

(The In my world series)
ISBN 0-86505-060-0

1. Identity (Psychology) – Juvenile literature.
2. Self –Juvenile literature. 3. Emotions –
Juvenile literature. I. Title. II. Series.

BF697.K34 1985   j155.2

To Samantha

350 Fifth Avenue
Suite 3308
New York, N.Y. 10118

102 Torbrick Avenue
Toronto, Ontario
Canada M4J 4Z5

Contents

Happy to be me

People are different in many ways.
We look different.
We like to do different things.
We can do some things well
and some things not so well.

We are the same in many ways too.
We all feel happy and sad.
We all laugh and cry.
We all have people whom we love
and who love us.
Being just the way we are makes us special.

We're special, can't you see?

There's no one in this whole wide world
Exactly just like me.
I am me and you are you,
We're special, can't you see?

I like to run and climb and slide,
I love to play outside.
I feel so free, just being me,
In the sun and wind and tide.

I can reach up to touch the sky,
Or curl into a ball.
I can stretch tall and I can bend
Into any shape at all.

Picture talk

Do any of the children look exactly the same?
How are they different in the things
they are doing?
What would it be like if all your friends
looked and acted exactly the same?
In what ways are you special?

5

We are all good at some things

I can climb a tree
as fast as a squirrel.
Well, maybe not quite that fast.
My daddy has to help me down from the tree.
I can play leapfrog.
I can walk on a log and not fall off.

I can't ride a bike yet.
I can't read or write.
But I can sing really well.
I like to sing with my friend Rosa.
Rosa has a lovely voice.

My friend Bryn can do cartwheels.
I can't.
My friend Julio can run fast.
I can't run as fast as he can.
Amanda can't do a handstand yet.
Her daddy is helping her.
Soon she will be able
to keep her legs up by herself.

I guess not everybody
can do everything well.
But everybody can do some things well.

Picture talk

What can the children in the picture do?
Which of these things can you do?
Which of these things are you learning to do?
What do you like to do when you go to the park?

The very best that I can do

Sally is watching me button my sweater.
She has buttoned her own sweater,
but she missed some buttons.
Sally is just learning to dress herself.

I used to miss buttons on my sweater too.
I did not miss them because I was little.
I missed them because I could not see well.
Now I wear glasses.
I find it easy to do things that
I used to find hard to do.
Now I can even help Sally with her buttons.

Dad is tying Joseph's shoelaces because
Joseph can't do them up yet.
Joseph is not as small as Sally.
He does not wear glasses as I do.
Joseph just needs extra time to learn.
He goes to a special school.
His teachers know how to help him
to do his best.

Ian is my oldest brother.
He is always in a hurry.
He makes mistakes when he does things quickly.
He is putting on his sweater backwards again!

Each one of us is different.
We find things hard to do for different reasons.
We cannot do everything perfectly,
but we do the very best that we can do!

Picture talk

Can you see what Sally has put on her dog's ears?
Can you see what she has put on her bear's paw?
Do you think Ian is doing his very best?

9

I was a baby once

Do you remember when you were born?
My brother Paul was born five days ago.
I am really glad to see Mommy again.
She has been in the hospital for almost a week.

I was a baby once.
Now I am big.
I can help to look after Paul.
My grandmother lives with us.
She can help too.
I just hope she will still have
time to play with me!

I have seen pictures of myself as a baby.
I had fat pink cheeks.
I didn't have any teeth.
I didn't have any hair.
My brother looks just like I did
when I was a baby.
He has fat pink cheeks.
He has no teeth.
He doesn't have any hair yet,
but he looks cute anyway!

At first I wasn't sure I wanted a baby brother.
Now I've changed my mind.

Picture talk

Do you know your baby facts?
Where were you born?
Were you born in the morning, afternoon,
evening, or at night?
When did you get your first tooth?
What was your first word?
When did you learn to walk?

11

I grew again

"Mom! Mom!
Somebody cut off the bottoms
of my favorite blue overalls.
I bet Jimmy did it.
He is always wrecking my stuff."

"Calm down, Shirley," Mom said.
"Jimmy didn't touch your pants.
You grew again. Can't you see?"

"I grew again! Oh boy!
I bet I can reach the cookie jar now."

Sometimes I stand beside Dad
to see if I have grown.
My nose touches his elbow now.
Sometimes I stand back to back
with my friends.
That's what my brothers are doing.

I know I have grown because now
I don't have to stand on the stool
to reach the sink.
How can you tell that you have grown?

Picture talk

Can you see how tall I am?
The middle blue line used to be mine.
Daddy hasn't measured us in a long, long time.
How much have I grown?
What is my brother doing to
make himself look taller?
What is the best way to measure
how tall you are?

Happy birthday to me

My name is Samantha.
Yesterday I was five.
I liked being five.

Today I am six.
It is my birthday.
Can you come to my party?
All my friends will be there.
We are going to wear party hats.
We will have cake and ice cream.
Have you ever played Blindman's Buff
or Pin the Tail on the Donkey?
They are my favorite games.
I love to be "it."

Birthdays are fun.
You get presents. You grow a year
older on each birthday.
You get to stay up later.
You also have to do more things!
You have to make your bed
and dress yourself.
I wonder if I'll like being six?

Picture talk

How did Samantha decorate
her house for the party?
What game are the children playing now?
What presents did you get on your last
birthday?
Do you have birthday parties?
What are your favorite games?
How do you decorate your house?

Changing as I grow

My name is Ridley.
This is a picture of me
when I was three.
I liked playing with big blocks
at nursery school.
I piled the blocks as high as I could.
I liked making big towers.
When the blocks fell down,
I piled them up again.

Now that I am six, I don't
play with blocks anymore.
I make snow castles in the winter.
I make people from modeling clay.
I make houses from popsicle sticks.

When I was small, I liked to play by myself.
I didn't want to share my toys.
Now I like to play with my friends.
I like to share my toys.

I am changing all the time.
I am getting older.
I am getting bigger.
I am learning new things each day.

Picture talk

How old is Ridley in this picture?
How old is he now?
What things does Ridley like to do
now that he is older?
How has Ridley changed?
How have you changed since you were three?
In what other ways do people change?

Watch what I can do

When I was small,
I could only crawl.
Then I learned to walk
And I learned to talk.
Now I can run
And have more fun.
I can ride a bike
As fast as I like.

My name is Arnie. Can you see me?
My sister Ruth and I are getting
new bicycles.
Our old bicycles are too small for us now.
Two years ago, I could not ride
a bicycle well.
Now I do not wobble when I ride.

Do you see my brother Joshua?
He has a small bicycle.
It used to be mine.
I am too big to ride it now.
I gave it to Joshua.
He gave away his tricycle.
It was too easy for him to ride.
He says, "Tricycles are for babies."

Joshua's bicycle has two extra wheels.
They are called training wheels.
Training wheels help Joshua to balance.
Soon Joshua will be able to balance on
only two wheels.

What can you do now?
What are the things you can do now that
you could not do when you were smaller?

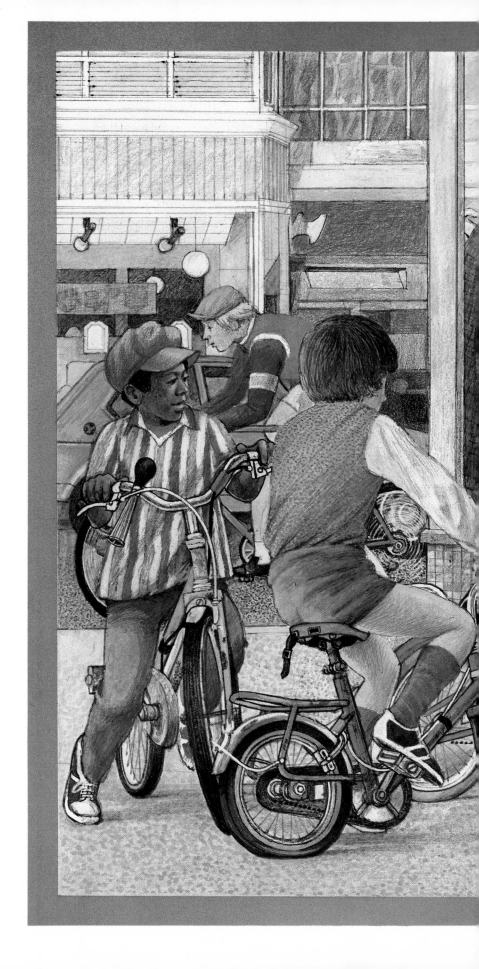

I am learning all the time

When I started school,
I knew how to write my name.
Do you know how to write your name?
Every day I learn new things at school.
I am learning the letters of the alphabet.
Soon I will be able to read the words.

My teacher makes it fun to learn.
She reads stories to us.
She lets us make up our own stories.
She plays games with us.
She helps us to make things.
Sometimes we dance and sing songs.
I like my teacher.
I like school.

I learn things outside of school too.
Last week at the Science Center,
I learned about bees.
Last night I learned about whales
from a program on television.
My friend Salim taught me how to
play Snakes and Ladders.
My mom showed me how to
tie my shoelaces.

Picture talk

What activity centers can you see in this
classroom?
How is this classroom the same as
your classroom?
How is it different from your classroom?
What things do you learn when you are
not in school?

I have many feelings

Sometimes I feel happy.
Sometimes I feel sad.
Today I felt very embarrassed.
I rode my bicycle into a fruit stand.
The accident was my fault.

My mother said, "Thank goodness."
She put her arm around me.
She was relieved that I wasn't hurt.
The owner of the fruit stand was angry.
He shouted at me. He waved his arms.
His face went red.
His wife felt sorry for me.

Sally was frightened.
She hid behind her mother's dress.
She peeked out at me.
Sally's mother said, "Oh, no!"
She was surprised to see the accident.
Everyone in the street was curious.
They stopped to look at us.

Can you see Jumy and Sang giggling?
How did they feel when they
saw me sitting on the tomatoes?
How would you have felt
if you had seen me crash?

Picture talk
What do the bodies and faces of the people
in the picture tell us about how they feel?
How can you tell that the boy who had the
accident is embarrassed?
Which people are angry, scared, upset,
or surprised?

My responsibilities

My family lives in a townhouse.
I share a room with my brother Masa.
My sister has her own room,
but she likes to play in ours.
Our room is bigger.
We even have an extra bed so a
friend can sleep overnight in our room.

Now that I am six,
I have more jobs to do.
Growing older means being more responsible.
Being more responsible means
I can do more things by myself.
I make my own bed.
I clean my carpet.
I also empty the garbage cans
and set the table.
My sister Norimi helps to tidy up.
Masa likes to help too,
but sometimes he plays instead.

Being six is more work.
It is also more fun.
I like helping my mother.
It makes me feel grown-up.
It makes me feel good.
It makes my mother happy.
I can't wait until I'm seven!

Picture talk

What jobs have the children finished doing?
What jobs do the children still have to do?
What are some of the things you can
do to help around your home?

When I grow up

What will I do when I grow up?
What will I learn and see?
Will I be a teacher or a carpenter?
Will I start my own family?
I could write a book or fly a plane
Or I might even predict the rain.

Where will I go when I grow up?
What wonderful things will I try?
Will I be a doctor, a mechanic, a chef,
Or in a spaceship fly?
I could bandage your leg and patch up your nose,
Or wrap up your face until nothing shows.

My friends and I love playing pretend.
We enjoy our games from beginning to end.
Sometimes we quarrel over who gets to be what,
And sometimes we share and sometimes not.
Pretending to be big sure can be fun
Right here in the house or outside in the sun.

Picture talk

What are the children in the picture
pretending to be?
What are they using to help them pretend?
What do you want to be when you grow up?
Why do you think your choice is a good one?
What kind of work do your mother and father do?
Do you want to do the same job as one of your
parents? Why? Why not?

My two cultures

My name is Kaori. My family is Japanese.
We moved to this country when I was just a baby.
My sister Linda was born here, but my brother Kay
and I were born in Japan.

Some of my friends were born in other countries.
Stavros is from Greece. Juan is from Mexico.
Toyin is from Nigeria.

I am the same as my friends in many ways.
We learn the same things at school.
We play the same games at recess. We like TV.

My friends and I are different in some ways, though.
We come from different cultures.
Culture means living life in a certain way.
The food I eat, the way I dress, and the things
I like to do are all part of my culture.
Because I am from Japan, my family does many things
the way we did when we were in Japan.
Now we live in this country.
Now we are part of another culture.
We do some things in new ways.
We have two cultures.

At school, my friends and I speak English.
At home, I speak Japanese.
On Monday evenings, I take jazz dancing.
On Thursday evenings, I learn Japanese dancing.
I like being part of two cultures. It's fun!

A visit to Japan

Last year, my family visited Japan.
I was five years old. My little sister was three,
and my brother was seven.
In Japan, the third, fifth, and seventh
birthdays are special.
Families go to shrines to celebrate these birthdays.
Shrines are places where people pray.

When we visited Japan, we went to a shrine.
My parents gave thanks that my brother and sister
and I are healthy and happy.
After visiting the shrine, my parents gave us
special birthday gifts.